The Impact of 5G Technology

Exploring the Potential of Faster Connectivity and its Implications

By

Ronald J. Martin

Disclaimer

The information provided in this book is for general informational purposes only. While every effort has been made to ensure the accuracy and completeness of the content, the author makes no representations or warranties of any kind, express or implied, about the completeness, accuracy, reliability, suitability, or availability concerning the information, products, services, or related graphics contained in this book or any purpose.

Any reliance you place on such information is therefore strictly at your own risk. The author disclaims any liability for any loss or damage, including without limitation, indirect or consequential loss or damage, or any loss or damage whatsoever arising from the use of or reliance on this book.

It is advised to verify the accuracy and applicability of any information presented in this book independently. The inclusion of links or references to external sources does not necessarily imply a recommendation or endorsement of the views expressed within them.

The content presented in this book does not constitute professional advice. Readers are encouraged to consult with relevant professionals in specific fields for advice tailored to their individual circumstances.

This disclaimer is subject to change without notice. By using this book, you agree to the terms outlined in this disclaimer. If you do not agree to these terms, please refrain from using the book.

Table of contents

Introduction

In an era propelled by the relentless march of technological advancement, the arrival of 5G technology signifies a monumental leap forward in the evolution of connectivity. This book serves as a guide, navigating the unexplored realms of swifter communication and shedding light on the transformative potential inherent in the fifth iteration of wireless technology.

To fully comprehend the profound impact of 5G, one must embark on a historical journey through the archives of communication technologies. From the pioneering era of telegraphy to the groundbreaking emergence of telephony and the global connectivity facilitated by 4G LTE, each chapter in this historical saga lays the groundwork for the monumental leap that is 5G. Delving into this background is not merely an exercise in retrospection but an essential prerequisite for understanding the intricacies of 5G's architecture and the paradigm shift it brings to the very essence of our interconnected existence.

The transition from Morse code's rudimentary dots and dashes to the lightning-fast data transmission capabilities of 5G reflects humanity's unwavering determination to transcend spatial and temporal limitations. Traversing through the epochs of technology, readers gain a deeper understanding of the gradual advancements that converge into the high-speed, minimal-delay assurances of 5G. This introductory segment functions as a cerebral time capsule, transporting us through the annals of history to recognize the pivotal milestones that propel us to the forefront of wireless communication.

Significance of 5G Technology

The impact of 5G transcends mere improvements in download speeds or smoother streaming encounters. It signifies a monumental transformation in the technological landscape, ushering in a plethora of potentials that resonate throughout various sectors and facets of society. Beyond mere connectivity, 5G embodies empowerment, ingenuity, and the realization of a globally interconnected ecosystem.

In examining the profound impact of 5G, we uncover its potential to revolutionize various industries. Take healthcare, for instance, where the landscape is poised for a transformation, enabling remote surgeries and real-time patient monitoring to transition from mere possibilities to everyday practices. Similarly, smart cities are on the verge of a dramatic evolution, becoming hubs of efficiency, sustainability, and improved living standards, driven by the seamless integration of interconnected devices facilitated by the unmatched speed and responsiveness of 5G technology.

The realm of entertainment and media consumption is primed for a paradigm shift as well. Virtual and augmented reality, once hindered by lag and latency issues, are now empowered to provide users with immersive, lifelike experiences. Beyond entertainment, the influence of 5G extends to education, manufacturing, transportation, and various other sectors, weaving a tapestry of innovation that fundamentally reshapes our daily experiences.

Objectives of the Book

As we venture into this journey of understanding, it is essential to establish the guiding principles that will direct our exploration. The goals of this book are diverse but unified around the central aim of offering readers a comprehensive comprehension of 5G technology.

Our first objective is to clarify the technical complexities surrounding 5G. By dissecting the intricate framework, protocols, and benchmarks that form the foundation of this technology, we equip readers to comprehend not only the essence of 5G but also the mechanisms and rationales behind its capabilities.

Additionally, our investigation transcends mere technicality to encompass the societal, economic, and cultural facets of 5G. How does 5G reshape various industries? What economic prospects and hurdles does it introduce? In what ways does it influence our social dynamics and cultural landscapes? These inquiries form the core of our interdisciplinary examination.

Furthermore, this book aims to stimulate informed discourse. By offering a thorough understanding of 5G, we equip readers with the resources to participate in nuanced dialogues regarding its ramifications. From privacy issues and cybersecurity risks to ethical dilemmas and digital equity, the book fosters critical thinking and open conversation.

Essentially, this book aims to cultivate a comprehensive and nuanced comprehension of 5G technology. It serves as a guiding light, illuminating the pathways of accelerated connectivity and enabling readers not only to understand the current landscape but also to actively contribute to shaping the future influenced by the pervasive impact of 5G technology. As we embark on this voyage into uncharted territory, let the objectives delineated here act as our guiding compass, directing our intellectual expedition through the diverse terrain of 5G exploration.

Chapter 1

Evolution of Communication Technologies

Within the intricate maze of human advancement, the development of communication technologies emerges as a vital thread interwoven into the fabric of our collective history. This section navigates through the annals of time, delving into the epochs that precede the fifth iteration of wireless technology, known as 5G. Our journey is steered by two pivotal subtopics: Historical Overview and Advancements Leading to 5G.

Historical Overview

The narrative of communication technologies unfolds as a grand saga, spanning across centuries and transcending the confines of geographical boundaries. To grasp the significance of 5G, we embark on a journey that surpasses the limitations of the present, traversing through the historical landscapes shaped by human creativity and innovation.

The earliest forms of human communication were rudimentary, carried by the wind, conveyed through gestures, and inscribed onto primitive cave walls. As civilizations flourished, the necessity for more sophisticated methods of sharing ideas over long distances became apparent. Ancient civilizations like the Egyptians, with their hieroglyphs on papyrus, and the Greeks, employing smoke signals and homing pigeons, contributed to the evolution of communication methods.

The invention of the printing press in the 15th century heralded a revolutionary transformation, democratizing access to information and setting the stage for the Renaissance. Subsequently, the telegraph emerged in the 19th century, fundamentally altering long-distance communication by transmitting encoded messages through electrical wires. This era witnessed the encoding of messages into Morse code, represented by dots and dashes, facilitating communication across continents and collapsing the barriers of time and space.

The introduction of the telephone by Alexander Graham Bell in 1876 marked a pivotal moment in the evolution of communication. This groundbreaking invention revolutionized the way people communicated, profoundly impacting societal interactions and laying the groundwork for future technological advancements. As time progressed, the emergence of radio waves as a medium for broadcasting further transformed the communication landscape, creating a global platform for sharing voices and music.

In the mid-20th century, television emerged as a powerful medium for visual storytelling, bringing captivating narratives into the homes of people around the world. Meanwhile, satellites orbiting the Earth played a crucial role as silent guardians, facilitating global broadcasts and fostering international connectivity on an unprecedented scale. These significant milestones, engraved in the annals of history, paved the way for the digital revolution that would soon follow, shaping the trajectory of human communication and connectivity.

Advancements Leading to 5G

The journey towards 5G unfolds not as a swift sprint, but rather as a relay race, where each generation of communication technology seamlessly passes the baton to the next. As we approach the threshold of the fifth generation, it becomes crucial to recognize the pivotal exchange points that have propelled us forward.

The emergence of the third generation, known as 3G, marked a significant milestone with the introduction of mobile data capabilities, transcending traditional voice calls to enable data transmission. This era witnessed the dawn of mobile internet and the nascent stages of the interconnected world we inhabit today. Subsequently, the transition to the fourth generation, 4G LTE, marked a leap forward with its promise of high-speed data connectivity, ushering in an era of streaming services and widespread adoption of smartphones. The advent of 4G laid the foundational framework for the proliferation of data-intensive applications and services that have become indispensable facets of modern life.

However, the insatiable desire for swifter and more dependable connectivity surpassed the capabilities offered by 4G. This relentless demand spurred the necessity for a technological breakthrough – 5G. The advancements paving the way for 5G are not solitary occurrences; rather, they represent the culmination of a symphony composed over several decades.

Fiber-optic networks emerged as the fundamental infrastructure, boasting the capability to transmit data at the speed of light. Additionally, innovations such as Massive MIMO (Multiple Input Multiple Output) and beamforming technologies surfaced, facilitating a more efficient utilization of the available frequencies. Moreover, the spectrum itself became a contested arena, with the millimeter-wave spectrum proving instrumental in providing the necessary bandwidth to support the colossal data streams envisioned by 5G.

Furthermore, the intersection of cloud computing and communication technologies paved the path for edge computing, resulting in reduced latency and heightened network responsiveness. This development was crucial as the Internet of Things (IoT) expanded exponentially, introducing a myriad of interconnected devices that necessitated a communication infrastructure capable of managing the resulting surge in data volume.

These advancements serve as stepping stones propelling us towards the pinnacle of 5G's capabilities. They constitute the framework upon which the fifth generation of wireless technology is positioned to redefine the fundamental nature of communication. The transition from 1G to 5G transcends mere speed; it signifies a profound paradigm shift in how we connect, communicate, and perceive the world around us.

In essence, the evolution of communication technologies embodies a testament to human ingenuity, with each successive chapter building upon the groundwork laid by its predecessors. As we stand on the brink of the 5G era, it becomes apparent that this journey is not solely about the technology itself; it's about recognizing the intricate interplay between human innovation and the tools we create to navigate the expansive realms of communication.

Chapter 2

Understanding 5G Technology

Alright, let's delve into the realm of 5G – exploring its underlying mechanisms, the technical specifications driving its performance, and its comparative analysis with preceding generations.

Key Features and Components

At the core of 5G lies an array of essential features and components, each playing a vital role in the complex system that ushers us into an era of unparalleled connectivity.

Millimeter-Wave Spectrum: One of the distinctive characteristics of 5G is its utilization of the millimeter-wave spectrum, a departure from previous generations. By harnessing frequencies exceeding 24 GHz, 5G achieves remarkable data transfer rates. Nonetheless, these high-frequency waves present challenges, including limited coverage range and vulnerability to environmental obstructions. Addressing these obstacles is essential to ensure the smooth implementation of 5G networks.

Massive MIMO (Multiple Input Multiple Output): 5G utilizes Massive MIMO, a technology employing numerous antennas at both transmitting and receiving points. This allows for the simultaneous transmission of multiple data streams, resulting in significant enhancements in data throughput and network efficiency. Massive MIMO underscores 5G's pursuit of optimizing spectrum usage and augmenting capacity.

Beamforming: In order to address the constraints presented by millimeter waves, 5G utilizes beamforming, a technology that directs signals with precision towards specific recipients instead of dispersing them in all directions. This focused method improves signal robustness and reliability, alleviating the obstacles inherent in transmitting at higher frequencies.

Low Latency: A fundamental aspect of 5G is its exceptionally low latency, which is vital for applications demanding instantaneous responsiveness. By minimizing latency to mere milliseconds, 5G facilitates transformative possibilities, ranging from augmented reality applications to critical communications in healthcare and autonomous vehicles.

Network Slicing: Introduced by 5G, the groundbreaking concept of network slicing involves dividing a single physical network into numerous virtual networks. Each segmented "slice" is customized to fulfill the distinct demands of particular applications, accommodating a broad spectrum of needs spanning from extensive IoT installations to high-speed broadband offerings.

Edge Computing Integration: Acknowledging the significance of latency reduction, 5G seamlessly integrates with edge computing. By handling data closer to its origin, whether it's a sensor or a user device, 5G diminishes the time taken for data transfer, thereby augmenting the overall responsiveness of the system.

Understanding the essential characteristics and elements of 5G reveals a landscape of innovation, wherein each element contributes to the resilient structure of this revolutionary technology.

Technical Specifications

Examining the inner workings of 5G unveils a collection of technical specifications that form the foundation of its capabilities. These specifications serve as the framework for the architecture and standards that delineate the fifth generation.

Data Rates and Throughput: 5G marks a significant departure in data rates and throughput capabilities. With peak data rates reaching up to 20 Gbps, 5G surpasses its predecessors by several magnitudes. This remarkable surge in speed results in quicker downloads, uninterrupted streaming, and the capacity to accommodate a myriad of connected devices concurrently.

Frequency Bands: The distribution of frequency bands stands as a pivotal element within 5G's technical specifications. Spanning a wide spectrum, from sub-1 GHz for expansive coverage to millimeter waves for rapid data rates, 5G optimizes the usage of accessible frequencies. This adaptability facilitates customized deployments tailored to address distinct needs, whether it involves extending connectivity to rural areas or supporting densely populated urban networks.

Channel Bandwidth: 5G attains its impressive data rates by allocating broader channel bandwidths in comparison to its predecessors. Channel bandwidths of up to 100 MHz or greater enable the swift transmission of data, playing a pivotal role in achieving the gigabit speeds synonymous with 5G technology..

Modulation and Coding Schemes: The modulation and coding strategies employed by 5G play a crucial role in maximizing the effectiveness of data transmission. Utilizing sophisticated methods like Quadrature Amplitude Modulation (QAM) and advanced error-correction codes, 5G enhances the resilience and dependability of communication, particularly in demanding conditions.

Duplexing: 5G utilizes both Time Division Duplexing (TDD) and Frequency Division Duplexing (FDD) to enable bidirectional communication. This adaptable method caters to a wide range of scenarios, spanning from IoT applications with heavy uplink requirements to the symmetrical communication needs of virtual reality applications.

Network Architecture: Embracing a more adaptable and expandable network structure defines the essence of 5G. Built upon cloud-native principles, software-defined networking (SDN), and network function virtualization (NFV), it establishes a foundation for a dynamic, flexible infrastructure adept at accommodating the evolving requirements of various applications.

Examining these technical specifications reveals the engineering excellence that characterizes 5G. It represents more than just a speed upgrade; rather, it embodies a finely crafted fusion of frequencies, data rates, and architectures meticulously synchronized to usher in the next era of connectivity.

Comparison with Previous Generations

To understand the importance of 5G, it's essential to compare it with previous generations, each serving as a building block in the progression of wireless communication.

1G: Analog Cellular Networks

The initial generation featured analog cellular networks, laying the groundwork for fundamental voice communication capabilities. This era served as the cornerstone for the subsequent mobile revolution.

2G: Digital Communication Emerges

The introduction of digital communication in 2G not only improved voice clarity but also introduced the Short Message Service (SMS). This era set the stage for the mobile data revolution.

3G: Mobile Data Takes Center Stage

The third generation represented a significant transition towards mobile data by introducing high-speed internet access. Key features of this period included video calling, mobile internet, and an enhanced network infrastructure.

4G: The Era of Mobile Broadband

The advent of 4G brought mobile broadband into fruition. Increased data speeds, enhanced network capacity, and reduced communication latency paved the way for the proliferation of mobile applications and services prevalent in today's digital landscape.

5G: Unleashing the Potential

When juxtaposed with earlier generations, 5G emerges as a technological powerhouse. Its unparalleled data speeds, minimal latency, and capacity to support numerous devices concurrently set it apart. While 4G primarily addressed mobile broadband needs, 5G expands its scope to encompass a wide array of uses, including critical communications, IoT implementations, and augmented reality ventures.

The comparison underscores that 5G represents more than just an incremental advancement; it signifies a revolutionary breakthrough. It transcends mere improvements in download speeds or latency reduction; instead, it reshapes the fundamental concepts of connectivity. As we progress through successive generations, each iteration incorporates and enhances the strengths of its predecessors, ultimately converging in the complex landscape of 5G.

Therefore, comprehending 5G entails delving into its fundamental attributes, deciphering the technical intricacies dictating its functionalities, and recognizing the paradigm shift it signifies when contrasted with earlier generations.

Chapter 3

Impacts on Connectivity

Sure, let's delve into how 5G is revolutionizing connectivity. It's not merely an incremental improvement; it represents a significant leap forward. Here are the three primary ways 5G is reshaping the landscape: Enhanced Speed and Bandwidth, Reduced Latency Applications, and Integration with the Internet of Things (IoT).

Enhanced Speed and Bandwidth

Picture your current internet speed as a leisurely stroll in the park, and then, with 5G, it's akin to strapping on jet engines and soaring through the sky. This is the transformative effect of enhanced speed and bandwidth – a revolutionary shift that surpasses the boundaries of conventional connectivity.

The surge in speed is staggering. With 5G, we're discussing downloading an entire HD movie in mere seconds. It's not merely about expediting movie nights; it's about unleashing potentials that were previously hindered by slower speeds.

Streaming becomes smooth and uninterrupted, free from frustrating pauses during your favorite shows. Thanks to 5G's enhanced bandwidth, digital content flows seamlessly like a symphony, providing an immersive experience without interruptions.

Online gaming enters a new era, where lag and latency are distant memories. Enhanced speed guarantees that your actions are executed instantly, transforming the outcome of games into a reflection of skill rather than connectivity limitations.

Video conferencing transforms into a lifelike experience with vivid high-definition video, clear audio, and seamless real-time collaboration, revolutionizing remote connections. Whether for business meetings or personal catch-ups, 5G elevates virtual interactions to almost in-person experiences.

Industries undergo significant transformations. Healthcare, for instance, harnesses 5G's enhanced speed for telemedicine, facilitating remote surgeries and continuous patient monitoring in real time. Similarly, education breaks free from geographical constraints as students seamlessly access high-quality educational content.

Business undergoes a transformation with rapid transactions and augmented reality (AR) shopping encounters. The accelerated speed and expanded bandwidth of 5G cultivate a vibrant environment where creativity flourishes, laying the groundwork for the forthcoming technological advancements.

Low Latency Applications

Now, let's delve into latency – the duration it takes for data to move from one point to another. In the realm of connectivity, latency acts as an inconspicuous barrier that 5G completely removes. With 5G, it's not merely about diminishing latency; it's about practically eradicating it.

Consider 5G as a data time-traveling apparatus. Whether it's vital medical communication or split-second decision-making in self-driving cars, minimal latency is the crucial element enabling these functions.

Gaming emerges as an ideal arena for experiencing the benefits of low latency. The lag time between your input and the game's reaction is reduced to the extent that it becomes nearly imperceptible. In gaming circles, this transformation is revolutionary. It's not merely about achieving high scores; it's about the immersive, instantaneous involvement that low latency delivers.

The realm of autonomous vehicles has transitioned into actuality. Thanks to low latency, the exchange of information between a vehicle and its environment occurs instantaneously. This advancement isn't solely about convenience; it's about ensuring safety and laying the groundwork for a substantial transformation in transportation.

Low latency in healthcare facilitates remote surgeries, envision a scenario where a surgeon conducts an operation from a distant location with minimal delay. This isn't a plot from a futuristic novel; it's the imminent reality shaped by the advancements of 5G.

Emergency services experience a significant advantage with instantaneous communication. Whether it involves disaster management or ensuring public safety, low latency guarantees that vital information reaches the appropriate authorities without any delay.

The influence on augmented and virtual reality is groundbreaking. Virtual environments merge seamlessly with reality, and augmented experiences blur the lines between digital and physical domains. This isn't solely about entertainment; it's about reshaping our understanding and engagement with the surrounding world.

Internet of Things (IoT) Integration

Let's delve into the Internet of Things (IoT), a network of interconnected devices sharing data. While IoT has existed previously, 5G elevates it by acting as the cohesive force that seamlessly integrates these devices into a responsive ecosystem.

Envision a scenario where your refrigerator communicates with your grocery store, ensuring you never run out of essentials like milk. With 5G, IoT becomes the conductor orchestrating a symphony of interconnected devices, fostering a genuinely smart and responsive environment.

Smart cities leverage the potential of IoT and 5G. From optimizing traffic flow to enhancing energy efficiency, the integration of sensors and devices ensures urban areas operate with unprecedented effectiveness. This isn't merely about convenience; it's about promoting sustainability and resource management.

In agriculture, IoT and 5G collaborate to enable precision farming. Field sensors gather real-time data on soil conditions, moisture levels, and crop health. This data, transmitted swiftly and with minimal latency thanks to 5G, empowers farmers to make data-driven decisions, maximizing yields while minimizing environmental impact.

The healthcare sector experiences a profound transformation with the synergy of IoT and 5G. Wearable devices continuously monitor vital signs, transmitting data to healthcare providers instantly. This real-time monitoring not only elevates patient care but also facilitates early intervention, potentially saving lives.

Industrial processes become more streamlined and agile. IoT sensors deployed in manufacturing plants communicate seamlessly with each other and centralized systems, optimizing production schedules, anticipating maintenance requirements, and ensuring uninterrupted operations. This isn't just about boosting productivity; it's about ushering in the era of intelligent, adaptive industries.

Security and surveillance operations see significant enhancements through the fusion of IoT and 5G. Smart cameras and sensors have the capability to react promptly to potential threats in real-time, bolstering public safety measures. It's not merely about surveillance; it's about forging a proactive and intelligent security infrastructure.

The effects of 5G on connectivity are not just gradual enhancements; they represent a monumental change. Improved speed and bandwidth redefine our digital interactions, while low latency enables real-time applications that were once considered unfeasible. The integration of IoT reshapes the foundation of our interconnected world. As we traverse this transformative terrain, it's not merely about quicker downloads or immersive gaming; it's about embracing a future where connectivity becomes a catalyst for limitless opportunities.

Chapter 4

Exploring Applications and Use Cases

Okay, let's explore the captivating realm of practical applications ushered in by 5G. It's not solely about accelerated downloads; it's about how 5G is revolutionizing our encounters in healthcare, urban infrastructure, self-driving vehicles, and the immersive domains of virtual and augmented reality.

Healthcare

Healthcare is on the brink of a groundbreaking change, propelled by the transformative power of 5G as it fuels a multitude of innovative advancements.

Remote Surgeries: Imagine a situation where a proficient surgeon in a distant location conducts a critical surgery on a patient situated miles away. Thanks to the minimal delay and rapid connectivity provided by 5G, remote surgeries materialize. Surgeons can manipulate robotic tools with accuracy, and the communication feedback is so immediate that it creates the sensation of being physically present in the operating theater.

Real-Time Monitoring: Consistent, instantaneous monitoring of patients becomes a norm with 5G. Wearable gadgets integrated with sensors gather vital signs and promptly relay this information to healthcare professionals. This proactive strategy facilitates early identification of irregularities, swift intervention, and tailored patient care.

Telemedicine and Consultations: 5G enables the extensive implementation of telemedicine, surpassing geographical limitations and extending healthcare services to remote regions. Virtual appointments become immersive and high-quality, allowing patients to engage with healthcare providers effortlessly.

IoT in Healthcare: The integration of the Internet of Things (IoT) with 5G enhances the capabilities of healthcare systems. Intelligent medical devices and IoT sensors gather and transmit data continuously, forming detailed health profiles for patients. This interconnected network extends from smart medication trackers to linked prosthetic devices, revolutionizing the healthcare environment.

Smart Cities

Incorporating technology to enhance urban living, Smart Cities find a powerful partner in 5G, reshaping them into centers of efficiency, sustainability, and enhanced quality of life.

Intelligent Traffic Management: The low latency and instantaneous connectivity of 5G are crucial in transforming traffic management. Smart traffic lights adapt instantly to traffic conditions, while sensors offer real-time data for flexible route planning. This not only minimizes congestion but also promotes fuel efficiency and environmental conservation.

Efficient Energy Management: In a Smart City driven by 5G technology, energy consumption becomes a flexible and adaptive process. Smart grids effectively distribute energy, while IoT sensors monitor and regulate usage instantly. This results in optimized energy utilization, decreased wastage, and enhanced sustainability within urban areas.

Connected Infrastructure: All facets of a Smart City become interconnected via 5G. This encompasses waste management systems that signal when bins reach capacity, and smart streetlights that modulate brightness according to time and usage trends, transforming the city's infrastructure into a dynamic, interlinked grid.

Enhanced Public Safety: 5G enables Smart Cities to implement sophisticated public safety protocols. Surveillance cameras equipped with facial recognition and real-time analytics swiftly detect and address security risks. Emergency services receive immediate, detailed data, enhancing their ability to respond promptly and bolstering overall public safety.

Autonomous Vehicles

The arrival of Autonomous Vehicles heralds a transformative era in transportation, with 5G serving as the essential element in facilitating their smooth navigation, communication, and functioning.

Real-Time Communication: The ultra-low latency of 5G guarantees real-time communication between autonomous vehicles and their environment. This is crucial for passenger and pedestrian safety, as it enables immediate responses to evolving road situations, traffic changes, and possible dangers.

Precision Mapping: Autonomous vehicles depend on precise, regularly updated maps for navigation. With 5G, there's seamless data exchange between vehicles and centralized mapping systems, guaranteeing access to the latest and most accurate information for navigation purposes.

Cooperative Driving: 5G facilitates vehicle-to-vehicle communication, creating a network of collaborative drivers. This communication enables vehicles to synchronize actions, like merging into traffic or navigating intricate intersections, ensuring fluid and effective traffic movement.

Enhanced Safety Features: 5G elevates the effectiveness of safety features in autonomous vehicles, enhancing functions such as adaptive cruise control and collision avoidance systems. Through real-time communication and data sharing, these vehicles can promptly anticipate and address potential hazards.

Virtual and Augmented Reality

Virtual and Augmented Reality (VR and AR) introduce an era of immersive encounters, with 5G acting as the foundational support that propels these technologies to unprecedented levels.

Immersive Gaming: 5G's boosted speed and minimal latency elevate gaming experiences to unparalleled levels of realism and interaction. VR gaming achieves genuine immersion, with hardly any delay, creating an environment where the virtual realm seamlessly integrates with reality.

AR in Retail: 5G-enabled Augmented Reality revolutionizes the retail sector by enabling customers to preview products in their actual surroundings before buying. Whether virtually trying on apparel or previewing furniture placement in their homes, AR, powered by 5G, enhances the retail journey.

Remote Collaboration: 5G facilitates smooth remote collaboration via VR and AR, allowing for virtual meetings where participants experience being in the same room or collaborative design sessions where team members interact with 3D models instantly. The potential for remote collaboration is limitless.

Enhanced Healthcare Training: In healthcare, VR and AR technologies driven by 5G transform training methods. Medical professionals can partake in lifelike simulations, honing their skills by practicing surgeries or intricate procedures in a virtual setting. This not only boosts their expertise but also enhances patient care outcomes.

Chapter 5

Economic and Business Implications

Amidst the ever-evolving technological landscape, 5G emerges as a transformative force, impacting industries and unveiling a panorama of economic and business considerations. This chapter delves into the significant shifts in Industry Transformations, the diverse Opportunities and Challenges that surface, and the prevailing Global Market Trends shaping the business environment.

Industry Transformations

5G represents more than just a speed enhancement; it acts as a catalyst for transformative shifts across various industries, reshaping the landscape of business operations and competition.

Manufacturing 4.0: The manufacturing industry is experiencing a significant transformation through the adoption of 5G technology. The realization of Industry 4.0, featuring smart, interconnected factories, is becoming a reality. Machines, equipped with sensors, communicate instantly, streamlining production workflows, reducing operational interruptions, and improving overall productivity. This not only results in cost efficiencies but also enables agile and responsive manufacturing practices.

Smart Agriculture: The agricultural sector is embracing technological advancements, and 5G is driving the emergence of smart agriculture, marked by precision farming and data-driven strategies. In this new landscape, IoT sensors deployed in fields gather real-time data on soil quality, weather conditions, and crop health. Armed with this information, farmers can fine-tune irrigation practices, monitor crop health, and make informed decisions, leading to higher yields and a more sustainable approach to farming.

Healthtech Revolution: As previously mentioned, the healthcare sector undergoes a significant transformation propelled by 5G technology. Telemedicine gains widespread acceptance, facilitating seamless connections between patients and healthcare providers. Remote surgeries, made possible by the combination of low latency and high-speed connectivity, redefine the boundaries of healthcare services. Furthermore, wearable devices play a crucial role in continuous patient monitoring, supplying real-time data for proactive healthcare management..

Retail Reinvented: Retailers seize the potential offered by 5G to rethink how customers interact with their brands. Augmented Reality (AR) enriches in-store engagements, enabling virtual clothing trials or furniture previews in customers' homes. By combining 5G and IoT, smart stores emerge, automating inventory management and delivering tailored shopping experiences as standard practice.

Opportunities and Challenges

The arrival of 5G heralds a terrain abundant with prospects, yet it also presents a series of hurdles that businesses must surmount.

Opportunities

Innovation Acceleration: 5G speeds up the rate of innovation, offering a fertile environment for businesses to delve into fresh products and services. From augmented reality enhancements to innovative healthcare applications, the opportunities are extensive.

Enhanced Connectivity for Businesses: Enhanced connectivity provides businesses with smoother collaboration, remote work capabilities, and effective communication. This is especially vital in today's globalized business landscape, where teams and clients are often dispersed worldwide.

IoT-driven Business Models: The fusion of 5G and IoT introduces fresh business paradigms. Enterprises can harness data derived from interconnected devices to glean valuable insights, streamline operations, and craft bespoke offerings.

Challenges

Infrastructure Investment: Deploying 5G necessitates substantial investment in infrastructure. Companies encounter the challenge of upgrading their current networks and systems to fully leverage the capabilities of 5G, a process that can demand considerable resources.

Security Concerns: The heightened connectivity ushered in by 5G also amplifies security apprehensions. With a greater number of devices and systems interconnected, businesses must confront the imperative for strong cybersecurity protocols to safeguard sensitive information..

Regulatory Complexity: The implementation of 5G is contingent on regulatory frameworks that differ across regions. Negotiating this intricate terrain demands businesses to stay updated on regulatory shifts and compliance prerequisites, contributing an additional layer of intricacy to their operations.

Global Market Trends

The evolving adoption of 5G technology influences shifting market trends that shape the global business landscape.

5G Infrastructure Investments: Countries and telecommunications firms globally are making substantial investments in 5G infrastructure. This widespread initiative is propelled by the acknowledgment that 5G represents more than just a technological advancement; it serves as a fundamental element for maintaining economic competitiveness.

Emergence of Edge Computing: A significant trend in the realm of 5G is its integration with edge computing. Edge computing entails handling data nearer to its origin, thereby decreasing latency and improving system responsiveness. This trend is especially pertinent for applications demanding instantaneous data processing, such as IoT devices and autonomous vehicles..

The Rise of Smart Cities: 5G plays a crucial role in advancing the concept of smart cities. Urban centers worldwide are integrating 5G technology to boost connectivity, facilitate IoT applications, and enhance overall city administration. This trend isn't confined to developed areas; emerging economies are also embracing smart city initiatives to tackle urban issues.

Industry-specific Transformations: Various sectors are undergoing distinct changes with the integration of 5G. For instance, the automotive sector is transitioning to connected and self-driving cars, whereas the entertainment industry is harnessing 5G for improved streaming services and immersive content distribution.

Global Collaboration and Standards Development: The implementation of 5G involves international cooperation among industry stakeholders and standardization bodies. These entities collaborate to set universal standards, promoting compatibility and a unified global environment for 5G technology.

In summary, the economic and business impacts of 5G are diverse. It goes beyond mere speed enhancements, influencing the restructuring of sectors, unlocking fresh prospects, and addressing hurdles along the way..

Chapter 6

Regulatory and Security Considerations

In the dynamic realm of technology, the arrival of 5G heralds not just unparalleled connectivity but also a host of nuanced considerations that transcend mere technological progress. This section explores the intricate domain of Regulatory and Security Considerations, focusing on the regulations dictating the implementation of 5G technology and the critical need to address issues such as privacy and cybersecurity..

Policy Frameworks

The implementation of 5G technology is closely intertwined with regulatory frameworks that oversee its rollout worldwide. Governments and regulatory bodies wield significant influence in shaping the landscape in which 5G operates.

National Strategies: Throughout the world, governments are crafting comprehensive national strategies to guide the implementation of 5G technology. These strategies encompass various aspects, including spectrum allocation and fostering private sector investment in infrastructure. National policies play a crucial role in fostering an environment conducive to the development and widespread adoption of 5G.

Spectrum Allocation: Assigning spectrum frequencies is pivotal in the deployment of 5G. Governments, alongside regulatory bodies, determine how spectrum bands are allocated to telecom operators. Achieving a balance between optimizing spectrum efficiency and fostering fair competition among operators is a delicate yet essential endeavor.

Infrastructure Development: Policy makers are proactively engaged in facilitating the essential infrastructure for 5G. This entails establishing a regulatory framework that incentivizes private sector investment in deploying 5G networks. Measures such as incentives, subsidies, and regulatory frameworks contribute to expediting the construction of the necessary infrastructure.

Interoperability and Standards: Standardization and interoperability are crucial in the realm of 5G. Policymakers participate in international collaborations to set uniform standards, guaranteeing smooth communication among devices and networks worldwide. This collective endeavor is vital for building a unified global ecosystem for 5G technology.

Privacy Concerns

As 5G technology ushers in an era of increased connectivity, it also raises substantial privacy concerns that require careful consideration and proactive steps.

Data Collection and Consent: The rise in IoT devices and enhanced connectivity enabled by 5G leads to an unprecedented volume of data generation, prompting apprehensions about its collection, storage, and utilization. Clear protocols for data collection and ensuring users provide informed consent emerge as essential strategies in addressing these apprehensions.

Surveillance and Monitoring: The advanced functionalities of 5G, such as instantaneous communication and minimal latency, prompt apprehensions about potential misuse, particularly for surveillance. Policymakers are tasked with the delicate balancing act of harnessing 5G's advantages while safeguarding individual privacy. Establishing legal frameworks becomes imperative to govern the scope of permissible surveillance activities.

Cross-Border Data Flow: The expansive reach of 5G networks entails the cross-border transmission of data, prompting inquiries regarding jurisdiction and the enforcement of data protection regulations. Policymakers are compelled to tackle these complexities to establish a unified approach to privacy within the interconnected framework of 5G.

Security of Personal Devices: With the proliferation of personal devices within the 5G ecosystem, ensuring the security of these devices emerges as a pivotal element in upholding user privacy. Collaboration between policymakers and industry players is essential to define security protocols that protect user data on smartphones, wearables, and various interconnected devices..

Cybersecurity Challenges

The interconnectivity inherent in 5G networks brings forth a multitude of cybersecurity hurdles that require a vigilant and adaptable strategy.

Network Vulnerabilities: The heightened complexity and interconnectedness of 5G networks expose potential vulnerabilities that malicious entities could exploit. Policymakers aim to identify and mitigate these vulnerabilities by implementing regulatory frameworks that enforce stringent security protocols for network operators.

Supply Chain Security: The international supply chain for 5G infrastructure elements brings forth cybersecurity vulnerabilities. Policymakers are wary of the possibility of tainted components infiltrating network infrastructure. Hence, rigorous security measures and thorough vetting processes for the supply chain are vital aspects of policy frameworks.

Emerging Threat Landscape: Policymakers need to anticipate and address the evolving threat landscape in the era of 5G. This involves preparing for potential new forms of cyberattacks, particularly those aimed at the vast array of IoT devices linked to 5G networks. Having adaptive cybersecurity policies is essential for effectively managing these emerging threats.

Public-Private Collaboration: Tackling cybersecurity challenges necessitates cooperation between public and private entities. Policymakers collaborate with industry partners to develop protocols for sharing information, responding to incidents, and working together to bolster the overall cybersecurity resilience of 5G networks.

In summary, managing the regulatory and security aspects of 5G requires a careful equilibrium between promoting innovation and protecting crucial elements like privacy and cybersecurity. Policy frameworks are crucial in guiding the rollout of 5G, addressing emerging challenges, and ensuring that its transformative benefits are harnessed securely and responsibly. As the world embraces the era of 5G connectivity, the development and refinement of strong regulatory frameworks will be pivotal in shaping the trajectory of this game-changing technology.

Chapter 7

Social and Cultural Impacts

As 5G technology permeates through the fabric of connectivity, its impact transcends mere technological advancements, molding and reshaping the social and cultural dynamics. This section delves into the significant effects of 5G on society and culture, examining shifts in communication habits, the necessity of digital accessibility, and the ethical dilemmas arising amidst heightened connectivity.

Changes in Communication Patterns

The arrival of 5G marks the opening of a fresh chapter in the realm of communication, reshaping the methods through which individuals and societies engage and communicate with one another.

Real-Time Communication: One distinguishing characteristic of 5G is its exceptionally low latency, enabling real-time communication that surpasses the constraints of earlier iterations. Video calls, online gaming, and collaborative work settings seamlessly unfold with minimal delays, fostering a feeling of instant engagement and connection.

Enhanced Connectivity: The improved velocity and dependability of 5G revolutionize communication dynamics. Expectations shift towards seamless high-definition video streaming, crystal-clear voice calls, and immediate file transfers, enriching the communication milieu with a heightened level of immersion. This transition not only reshapes personal exchanges but also carries significant implications for business communication and collaborative endeavors.

Rise of Augmented Reality (AR) and Virtual Reality (VR): 5G enhances the potential of AR and VR applications like never before. Picture attending virtual meetings where participants experience a physical presence in the same room or delving into immersive virtual realms for educational and entertainment purposes. These technologies redefine communication dynamics, introducing fresh avenues for engagement and interaction.

Ubiquitous Connectivity: The commitment of 5G to universal connectivity implies that individuals are no longer confined by geographic limitations. Regardless of whether they are in urban hubs or remote regions, people can maintain uninterrupted connections, closing geographical divides and nurturing a perception of a globally linked society.

Digital Inclusion

As the global community embraces the possibilities of 5G, the importance of digital inclusion becomes increasingly evident, aiming to bridge the gaps in access and guaranteeing that the advantages of connectivity are accessible to all sectors of society.

Closing the Connectivity Gap: 5G holds the promise of narrowing the digital gap by providing fast connectivity to regions that were historically underserved. This has the potential to empower communities in remote areas, granting them access to educational materials, telemedicine services, and economic prospects that were previously inaccessible.

Accessibility for All: Promoting digital inclusion in the era of 5G entails tackling accessibility concerns. This includes developing user interfaces that accommodate various needs and integrating features that aid individuals with disabilities, ensuring that technology is accessible and functional for all.

Rural Empowerment: Rural areas are poised to benefit greatly from the advent of 5G. Beyond just better connectivity, 5G has the potential to drive economic growth, expand educational access, and make vital services such as healthcare more accessible. This fosters greater empowerment among rural communities as a whole.

Education for All: The implementation of 5G has the potential to transform education by providing students worldwide with access to high-quality content and interactive learning opportunities. Virtual classrooms, distance learning, and collaborative educational platforms emerge as effective means of democratizing education, breaking down geographical limitations.

Ethical Considerations

The revolutionary impact of 5G brings forth ethical considerations that require thoughtful contemplation and proactive measures to navigate the intricate interplay of technology, society, and culture.

Privacy in the 5G Era: The considerable volume of data produced by devices connected to 5G raises privacy apprehensions. Collaboration between policymakers and industry players is essential to develop strong privacy protocols safeguarding user data, guaranteeing consent, and thwarting unauthorized access.

Security and Trust: The interconnectivity inherent in 5G networks amplifies security apprehensions. Establishing and upholding trust within the 5G framework necessitates strong cybersecurity protocols, transparent operations, and mechanisms for holding parties accountable in case of security breaches.

Algorithmic Bias and Fairness: As 5G integrates artificial intelligence (AI) and machine learning (ML) into diverse applications, the concern of algorithmic bias emerges. Ethical considerations entail rectifying biases within algorithms to uphold fairness and prevent discriminatory results, particularly in critical sectors such as healthcare, finance, and employment.

Environmental Impact: The broad implementation of 5G infrastructure prompts inquiries into its environmental repercussions. Ethical considerations encompass reducing the carbon footprint of 5G networks, responsibly handling electronic waste, and ensuring that technological advancements align with environmental sustainability objectives.

Inclusivity and Diversity: The advancement and application of 5G technologies should adhere to principles of inclusivity and diversity. Ethical considerations include ensuring equitable distribution of 5G benefits, avoiding the amplification of current social disparities, and advocating for diversity in technology development and decision-making processes.

Community Engagement: Ethical considerations during the 5G era encompass community engagement. When implementing 5G infrastructure, it's vital for stakeholders to involve local communities, acknowledge cultural sensitivities, and evaluate the social impacts of technological advancements. This entails promoting inclusive decision-making processes that incorporate diverse perspectives and foster collaboration.

In essence, the societal and cultural effects of 5G extend beyond mere technological progress, encompassing shifts in how we communicate, the necessity of ensuring digital access for all, and the ethical principles guiding its responsible adoption. As we embrace the age of 5G connectivity, it's crucial to recognize and address these impacts to ensure that the advantages are distributed equitably, ethically, and with an eye toward sustainability.

Chapter 8

Future Prospects and Emerging Technologies

As 5G technology solidifies its role as a catalyst for change, permeating communication, industries, and societies, attention naturally shifts towards the potential on the horizon. This chapter delves into the Future Prospects and Emerging Technologies, examining what lies beyond the present state of 5G, the advancements that will mold the technological terrain, and the innovations positioned to reshape how we connect, communicate, and perceive our surroundings.

Beyond 5G Developments

Although 5G represents the current zenith of wireless communication, the dynamic nature of technology urges us to look towards what lies ahead. The trajectory of Beyond 5G developments offers an intriguing path that leverages the successes and tackles the challenges of the current generation.

6G and the Terahertz Frontier: The forthcoming evolutionary phase, sometimes termed as 6G, is anticipated to operate within the terahertz frequency spectrum. This advancement holds the potential for further elevated data rates, reduced latency, and expanded capacity. Terahertz communication introduces prospects for applications spanning from advanced augmented reality encounters to instantaneous holographic communication.

Quantum Communication: Looking past 5G, quantum communication emerges as an innovative frontier leveraging principles of quantum mechanics to fortify and advance communication. Quantum key distribution (QKD) has the capability to transform data security by employing inherent properties of quantum particles for secure key exchange, effectively thwarting eavesdropping attempts.

Integrated Satellite Communication: In forthcoming communication networks, satellites are anticipated to play a more integrated role, especially with the emergence of Low Earth Orbit (LEO) satellite constellations. When paired with advanced signal processing, these constellations hold the potential to augment global connectivity significantly. This integration could prove instrumental in bridging connectivity disparities in remote regions and during emergency situations.

Bio-Inspired Communication Systems: Future communication technologies may take cues from biological systems, aiming to replicate the efficiency and adaptability observed in nature. This approach could result in the creation of self-organizing networks that are resilient to disturbances and capable of adjusting to changing environmental factors. By emulating nature's mechanisms, wireless communication could achieve a heightened level of resilience and robustness.

AI-Enhanced Communication Networks: AI is positioned to have a pivotal role in the advancement of communication networks. In the post-5G era, AI algorithms will be crucial for enhancing network efficiency, preempting and addressing issues, and tailoring services according to user preferences. This heralds the arrival of intelligent, self-adjusting networks.

Innovations on the Horizon

Technological innovations extend well beyond communication protocols, encompassing a wide range of advancements that are set to define our technological landscape in the future.

Edge Computing Evolution: Expanding upon the fusion of 5G and edge computing, upcoming innovations concentrate on advancing the functionalities of edge computing frameworks. This progression entails bringing computational power nearer to the data source, facilitating instantaneous processing for various applications, including augmented reality and Industrial Internet of Things (IIoT).

Extended Reality (XR): As 5G evolves, Extended Reality (XR) technologies, which include Augmented Reality (AR), Virtual Reality (VR), and Mixed Reality (MR), are poised for significant advancements. With improved data rates and reduced latency, XR applications will provide more lifelike and immersive experiences, influencing sectors like gaming, education, healthcare, and remote teamwork.

Biometric Authentication: Advancements in biometric authentication technologies will be crucial for enhancing secure and user-friendly interactions. Future progressions might involve sophisticated biometric methods like continuous authentication utilizing behavioral patterns, more accurate facial recognition, and the integration of biometrics into various applications beyond conventional security measures.

Robotics and Autonomous Systems: The ability of 5G to facilitate low-latency communication serves as the cornerstone for advancing robotics and autonomous systems. Developments in this domain entail collaborative robots (cobots) seamlessly working alongside humans, autonomous vehicles navigating intricate surroundings, and drones executing tasks with unprecedented levels of autonomy and precision.

Smart Infrastructure and Cities: Future advancements also extend to the domain of smart infrastructure and urban development. Sophisticated sensors, interconnected devices, and real-time data analytics will play crucial roles in establishing intelligent urban ecosystems. These innovations may encompass optimized energy utilization, dynamic transportation networks, and the integration of technology to elevate the overall quality of life in cities.

Space-Based Internet: Advancements in space-based internet technologies offer the potential for a paradigm shift in global connectivity. Initiatives focusing on deploying extensive satellite constellations in low Earth orbit aspire to deliver high-speed, low-latency internet connectivity to areas lacking adequate access, thereby fostering greater global interconnectedness.

Furthermore, the future prospects and emerging technologies beyond 5G offer a compelling narrative of innovation and metamorphosis. Ranging from communication systems operating in the terahertz spectrum to leveraging quantum principles for secure communication, the trajectory unfolds with promises of enhanced capabilities and novel applications. Anticipated innovations span diverse domains, including AI-driven networks, extended reality experiences, advanced biometrics, robotics, smart cities, and the democratization of internet access through space-based technologies. Standing at the threshold of this technological frontier, the journey beyond 5G holds the promise of new possibilities and the potential to redefine our interactions with and perceptions of the world.

Conclusion

As we conclude our journey delving into the realm of 5G technology, this book has unveiled a narrative of significant change, where the strands of connectivity create a rich fabric that stretches beyond the current moment into the vast landscape of potentialities. As we draw this expedition to an end, let's contemplate the fundamental insights and consider the ramifications echoing through the halls of technological progress.

Recap of the Journey

Our expedition commenced with the excitement surrounding 5G's promise of accelerated connectivity, but quickly evolved into an exploration of its diverse impacts. From the restructuring of communication dynamics to the transformation of various industries, the societal changes, and the intricate interplay of regulatory factors, each chapter peeled back another layer of the complex tapestry that is 5G.

Within the realms of industries, we observed the profound changes ushered in by 5G – from highly efficient smart factories to healthcare breaking down geographical barriers, and cities embracing the onset of a truly interconnected age. The societal and cultural landscape experienced a shift, where communication transcended mere transmission to become an immersive experience, promoting inclusivity and prompting ethical considerations.

The chapters explored the intricate regulatory frameworks and security hurdles, highlighting the nuanced equilibrium between innovation and accountability. From the economic repercussions molding industrial frameworks to the pivotal position of 5G in laying the groundwork for tomorrow, our expedition underscored the extensive impact of connectivity.

Final Contemplation

As we stand at the intersection of the present and the future, the reverberations of 5G extend far beyond its technological framework. The chapters have illuminated a pathway toward a future defined by innovations that transcend the boundaries of our current understanding.

The trajectory of connectivity's evolution isn't merely linear but rather a quantum leap into unexplored realms. The advancements beyond 5G beckon us with promises of terahertz frequencies, quantum communication, integrated satellite networks, and the symbiotic fusion of AI with telecommunications infrastructure. The forthcoming innovations, spanning from edge computing to augmented reality, biometric systems, robotics, smart urban environments, and space-based internet, depict a landscape where technology seamlessly intertwines with the very fabric of our existence.

In this final reflection, our exploration's narrative seamlessly merges into a contemplation of the ongoing saga—a narrative of a connected world where technological progress aligns with our shared aspirations for advancement, inclusivity, and a brighter tomorrow.

As we draw this chapter to a close, the book not only chronicles the trajectory of technological evolution but also extends an invitation—an invitation to embark on the unfolding journey of the future with a spirit of inquiry, accountability, and a readiness to contribute to the narrative of connectivity. The voyage beyond these pages is a continuation—an odyssey where the potentialities are as limitless as humanity's capacity to envision, innovate, and establish connections. May the forthcoming era bear witness to the collaborative ethos that propels us towards a connected world that enhances lives, transcends barriers, and embraces the infinite possibilities of the morrow.

Leaving a Review

Dear Reader,

I trust this message reaches you in good spirits. I wanted to extend my heartfelt appreciation for selecting this book. It's been quite a journey, and I genuinely hope you discovered it to be enlightening and worthwhile.

As an author, your input holds significant value for me. I would deeply appreciate it if you could spare a moment to provide your thoughts and impressions by leaving a review on the platform where you obtained the book.

Your review offers valuable insights for me and assists other readers in discovering the book, helping them determine if it suits their preferences and requirements. Whether you share a brief summary or provide a more elaborate evaluation, your honest feedback is immensely valued.

Once again, thank you for joining me on this journey. I eagerly anticipate hearing your thoughts and sincerely value the time and consideration you've given.

Warm regards,
Ronald J. Martin